The Wonderful Wisdom of Ants

PHILIP BUNTING

CROWN BOOKS
for Young Readers
New York

This is an ant.

And this is an ant.

And this is an ant.

And this is an ant. And this is an ant. And this is an ant.

And this is an ant.

 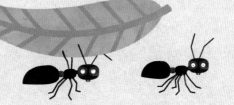 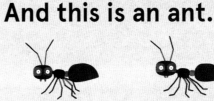

And this is an ant. And this is an ant. And this is an ant.

And this is an ant.

And this is an ant. And this is an ant. And this is an ant.

And this is an ant.

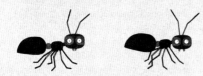 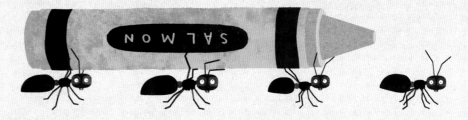

And this is an ant. And this is an ant. And this is an ant.

of these little girls and guys on our planet.
Roughly.

If you weighed all those ants,
they would weigh the same as
all the humans in the world.

Roughly.

Ants love:

Family.

Micronaps.

Recycling.

Thanks!

You're welcome.

Helping others.

Being caught on camera carrying stuff way bigger than they are.

Ants do not love:

Kettles.

Boots.

Magnifying glasses.

Anteaters (obviously).

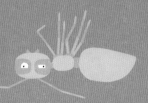

The cold.

Just as we live in
groups (like families,
schools, or cities), ants exist
as part of their colony.
They rely on other ants to gather
food, build the nest, and raise
the next generation of baby ants.
In turn, each little ant does
its best for those around
it, rather than
for itself.

All ant colonies start with one queen-to-be . . .

Moi?

who takes her
nuptial flight . . .

and then finds a nice spot
to lay some tiny ant eggs.

These eggs quickly
develop into larvae . . .

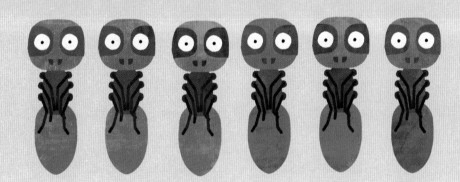

which soon grow
to become pupae.

And before you can say "Bob's your ant,"
a new colony has begun.

Colonies can be tiny, like our villages, or huge,
like our cities. But unlike our communities,
all the ants in a colony are one big family.

Little help?

From the moment they hatch, each ant knows its job and is perfectly suited to its role in the colony.

Queen.
Female.
Founds the colony.
Lays eggs.
Lays eggs.
Lays eggs . . .

Worker.
Female.
Finds food.
Maintains nest.
Cares for baby ants.
Lays no eggs.

Soldier.
Female.
Protects the colony.
Expands nest.
Finds food.
Lays no eggs.

Drone.
Male.
Does no housework.
Takes to the sky.
Reproduces.
Drops dead.

Princess.
Female.
Queen-in-waiting.
Mates with drone.
Founds new colony.
Lays eggs.

Living in such large families means that ants are naturally social little creatures. Their ability to get along and work with one another is the ants' superpower and allows them to do some wonderful things.

I'll be back in time for dinner.

For example, weaver ants hang on
to one another to build living bridges,
so that others from their colony
can cross from one tree to the next!
To be able to do things like this,
ants have developed their own
special way of communicating.

But unlike noisy humans, ants don't use sound to communicate—they chat through an odorous alphabet of smells. The letters of their aromatic ABC are called pheromones.

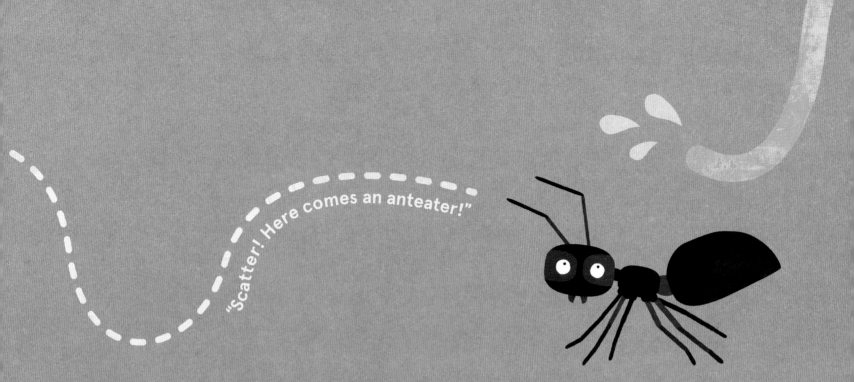

"Scatter! Here comes an anteater!"

"Quick! I found a patch of sprinkles!"

"I had a baked bean for breakfast."

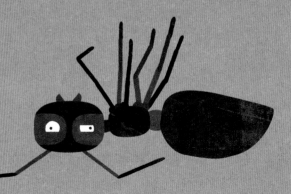

Here's how ants use pheromones to make the most of that patch of sprinkles. . . .

Act 1.
Worker ant leaves nest, comes across delicious pile of sprinkles, recently dropped from atop a doughnut (or possibly ice cream).

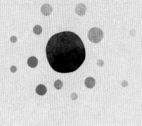

Act 2.
Worker quickly returns to nest with one sprinkle. She leaves a trail of fragrant instructions to lead others back to the sweet stuff.

"Sprinkles!" "Sprinkles!" "Sprinkles!"

Act 3.
The first worker tells her friends in the nest about the sprinkles by tapping and rubbing their antennae. Other workers follow the funky trail to investigate.

"Sprinkles!" "Sprinkles!" "Sprinkles!"

Act 4.
Each worker then takes a sprinkle back to the nest, leaving her own scent trail, helping more workers find their way to the mother lode.

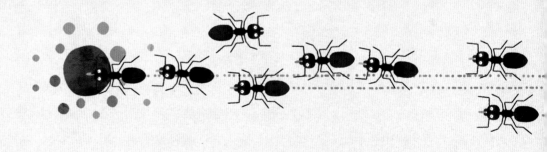

Act 5.
Eventually, no more sprinkles. The pheromone trails fade, and the workers store the sprinkles away for the good of the colony. Or so we think.

Sprinkle party!

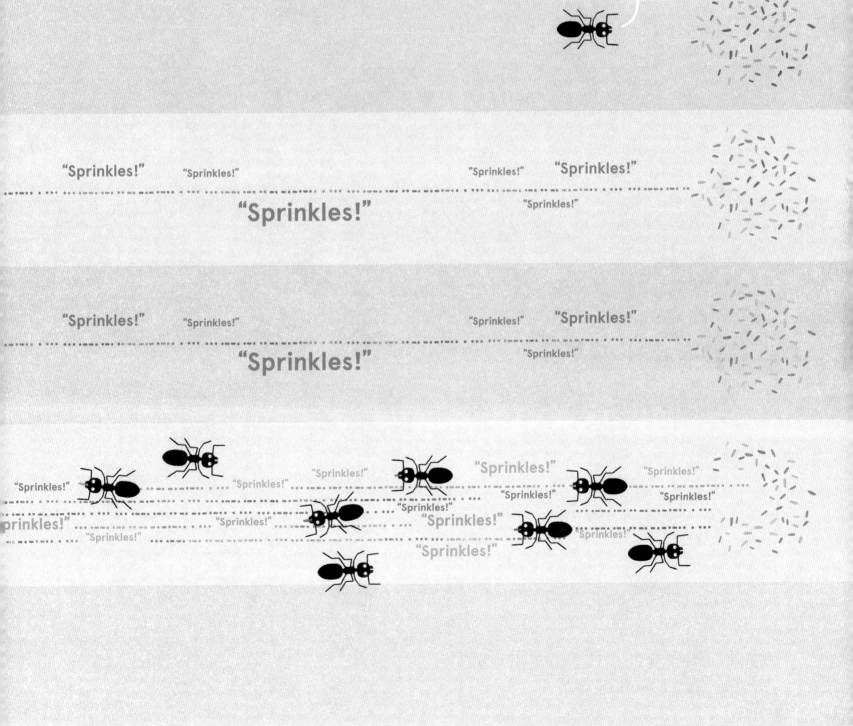

But beyond their clear love for sprinkles, ants are not fussy eaters. Most species are

om-

nom-

nom-

nom-

nom-

nom-
nivorous.

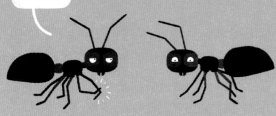

Ouch!

Or omnivorous, for short. Which means they will eat pretty much anything they can lay their mandibles on.

As they go about their day, ants recycle the nutrients of plants and trees to create richer soil, which benefits all life on Earth.

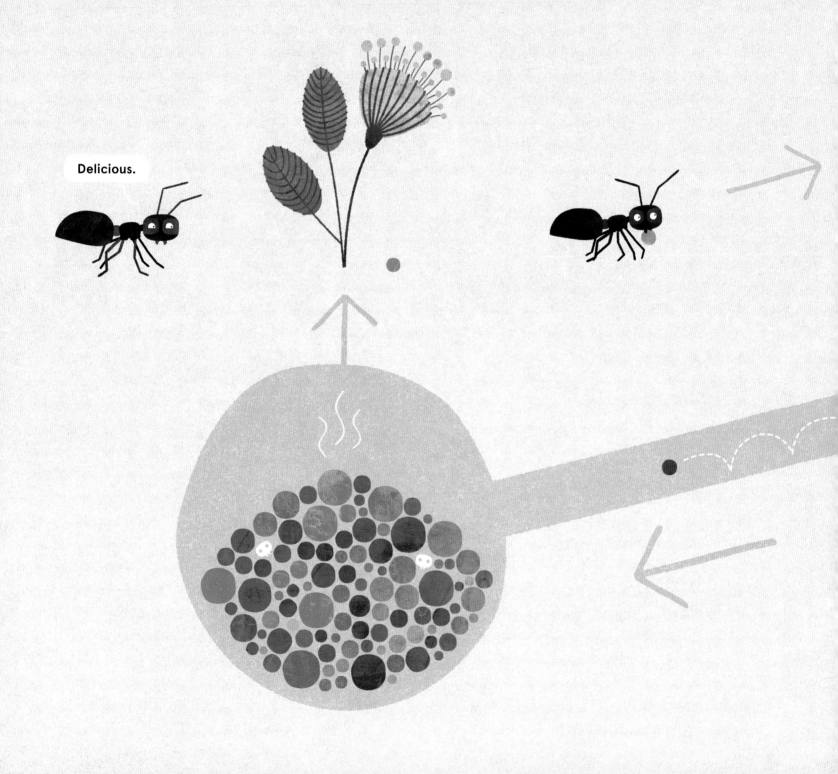

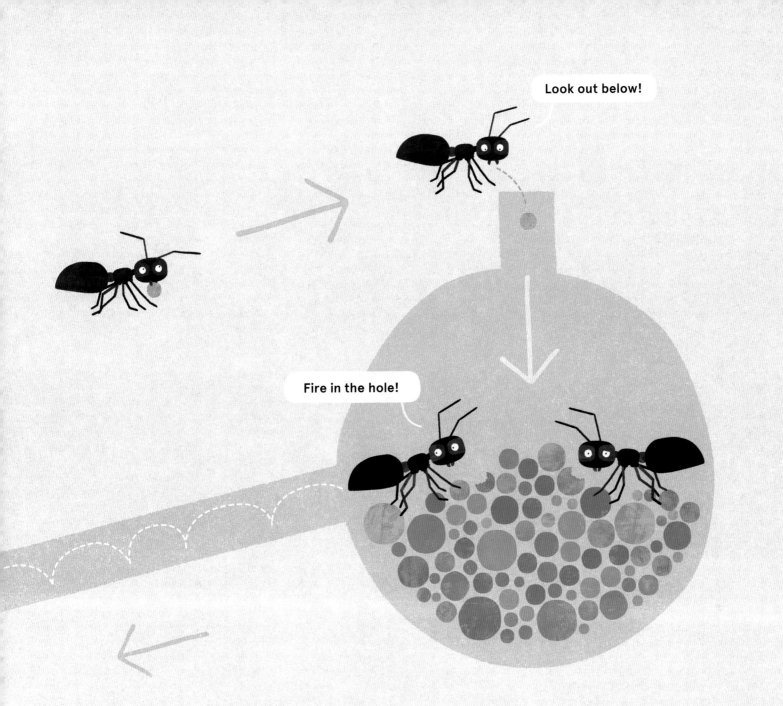

To ants, helping out the planet comes naturally. And they don't need fancy recycling bins to help them do it.

Okay, so ants may not make the world go round,
but they certainly make it a better place for
the rest of us. We can learn a lot from
these marvelous little creatures.

Love your family.

Reuse or recycle everything.
Waste nothing.

Power nap whenever possible.

Always do your best for
those around you.

And if you do all these things,
just like our six-legged friends, you will . . .

Leave the

in better

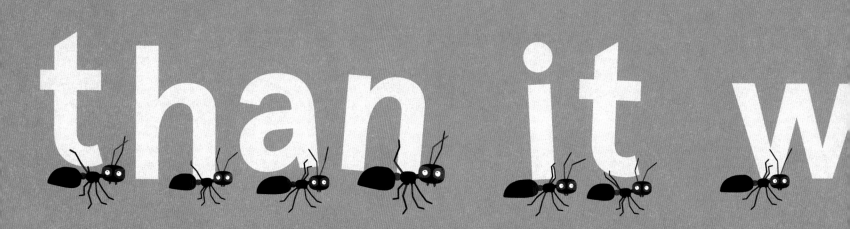

than it w

you ʙoot

Earth

shape

as when

here.

FOR MY ANTS: BERYL, JOYCE, JUDE + ROS

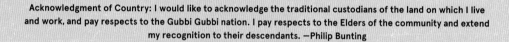

**Philip Bunting is not a myrmecologist.
He's not even an entomologist. Gasp.
Philip is just a keen dabbler who believes that
the answers to many of life's questions
can be found in your own backyard
(once you're ready to look).**

Acknowledgment of Country: I would like to acknowledge the traditional custodians of the land on which I live and work, and pay respects to the Gubbi Gubbi nation. I pay respects to the Elders of the community and extend my recognition to their descendants. —Philip Bunting

All rights reserved. Published in the United States by Crown Books for Young Readers, an imprint of Random House Children's Books, a division of Penguin Random House LLC, New York. Originally published by Scholastic Australia, Sydney, in 2020.

Crown and the colophon are registered trademarks of Penguin Random House LLC.

Visit us on the Web! rhcbooks.com

Educators and librarians, for a variety of teaching tools, visit us at RHTeachersLibrarians.com

Library of Congress Cataloging-in-Publication Data is available upon request.
ISBN 978-0-593-56778-4 (hardcover) — ISBN 978-0-593-56779-1 (lib. bdg.) — ISBN 978-0-593-56780-7 (ebook)

The text of this book is set in 20-point Apercu Bold.
The illustrations in this book were created using papercut and digital collage.

MANUFACTURED IN CHINA
10 9 8 7 6 5 4 3 2 1
First American Edition